LEAN IN:
Live from Everywhere

John R. Garry

ISBN-13: 978-0692481813
ISBN-10: 0692481818

Cover photo by J.R. Garry © 2015

To everyone standing in front of the stages and to those behind the Mics.
No one is free until we all are heard.
Everyone Lean In.

CONTENTS

ACKNOWLEDGMENTS

Heartfelt gratitude to the supporters and critical ears at Open Mics up and down the state of California, where all these pieces were born. When you are up at the front of a room, you can see and feel when people listen with their hearts. They *Lean In*. It is soul food and it makes this work more meaningful for me. These pieces have roots in my mind and in my soul but would not be what they are had the crowds not taken a moment to *Lean In*.

Informed Consent

Common things happen to common people in common places,
Still sanity is a hard state to maintain.
I don't write about extraordinary things happening to extraordinary people,
I write about the rise and fall of human experience.
I don't promise to make sense or use words correctly.
There is no guarantee you'll feel everything I say,
But one little connection is better than ignoring the feeling or the place in
your heart, mind, or soul, which is longing to be spoken to.
Just like all things, this too shall fade and pass.
The tragedy would be to not see and honor the 'you' in all things.

I am the reason people hate poets

I am the reason people hate poets
I am not clear, I am far from direct
Like my friend Lauren once said,
        "John, you're every angle but the right one."
I protest with emotion and not enough with actual logic or facts
I make references
To music no one listens to
Books no one has read

Really like Haiku
Poetry Re-fridge magnets
Open Mics sober

I carry a pen and paper everywhere
But I don't call myself a writer,
I'm a verbal vomiter.
I make words up,
I don't speak correctly,
Don't respect the rules of grammar
Or dictates that I stop wearing bow ties.
I use metaphor like old folks use the passing lane:
        Too often
        And poorly.
I am the reason people hate poets.
I can be ironic, self-effacing, and self indulgent
For instance:
I write bad poetry and I will still try to sell you my book.
I slept with your wives; my girlfriends have a history of depression and dad issues...
And I write about it.
Still, I am not a writer, but I am "wordy".
I am the reason people hate poets.
I make people think, but more often just frustrated.

    I end things without closure…

Did you hear what he said?

This is a day that has no answers. That the day comes with suicide and sweet wine makes no matter.
The cause and effect are years apart.

This is the start and the finish of what is and what was, the flurry of awareness is

about me, and had I not written about it, I may not even ½ known...

Where do the ages go?
Marked down one by one. Like sips from this glass, like pulls from this pipe, childlike and wise.

Rhythms of the Saints, heightened by the <u>ALL</u> that <u>THIS</u> is.
These bags are packed for every occasion.

Turpentine tortoises, these slow meandering evaporations I call memories.

These seedling thoughts, buried deep in the soils of my mind, pound their way out like they want out of an asylum.
Where proving your sanity is harder than showing your ill health.
In this insane world where broken feels normal,
We all must breathe and stop, breathe and stop (for real this time)
Breathe...

And in each one of these scenes
Plaster and brick, mortar and paint

All at the end of the world I know, which will grow and change the next instant, the questions remain unanswered.

What a world with tireless characters, unwavered by the evening wind, by these words from within.

Soldiers, singers, poets, muse and musicians,

Pulling the covers up to keep the monsters away- but we only lock them in!

The time has come to let the monster free-
Let him eat cookies AND carrots, wine AND cauliflower!

This remains a day with no answers, but as the scribbles grow larger, the time to

wrap this up begins...

And ends,

That's when I heard him say,

"It will give you the answer if you pay attention."

Robin Hood and Little John

LEAN IN

Robin Hood and Little John walking through the forest...

My childhood was gifted me
Skin color, private school and kind words
Saw the darkness when the shades were drawn
In schools of poor choices- innocence gone
Watching others struggle
Some had it tough, others too easy
Disillusioned by games of religion and democracy
Some lives fairways others potholes
Some swimming in freshness, others riding dirty
Waiting for the other shoe to drop

Never ever thinking there was danger in the water...

The community guns drawn, wagons already circled round dry grass, scorched
rights, anger embers
The American Dream is the disease, virus, cultural Ebola
Like Jordan's to the block, blankets on slave ships
Misdirection, David and this Goliath federal minefield
United we stand, but they would rather you kneel...
On grains of rice...
Mad at Muslim nations but the Supreme Court is the one suicide bombing
women's rights.
Trevon, Palestine, Isla Vista...
Humans killing humans will never be right
They say there is a bright day for every dark night
So, rage and hope fill these lines

Robin Hood and Little John running through the forest...

No more running, no more hiding. No more facebook or ear budding.
No more boozing or tweaking.
No more blinding by the light of your digital devices.
The Eyes will have it,
We will see the wedge cut lies stuck in every crooked policy,
So it only looks straight.
We want the basics for all people, all communities...
Land, bread, housing, education, clothing, justice and peace.
We will jump these fences with self-determination through resistance,
Dodging the beasts of burdens passed down from our forefathers,
Finding unity with others who share the burden of oppression

A Love Poem

LEAN IN

I cover you with butter and a touch of salt,
It is to you corn on the cob that my heart calls out.
Through your in seasons and out,
To you our native fruit the country is devout.
On a hot day, it is you ice pop when no one else will do.
On those sweaty nights, you lay cool in the freezer Mr. Otter Pop,
I will always love you.
I wouldn't be here today if the old school hadn't paved the way-
So I shout you out, the childhood staple,
Peanut butter and jell-ay!
I like you with the crusts or even without,
Cause PB and J you are always there when the rest of the grub has run out.
I would not have the same smile today,
If carnitas, taco trucks, or sopes had not been just around the way.
I've had you for breakfast lunch and dinner,
If I wasn't having you 3 to 4 times per week...
I'd be 3-4 pounds thinner.
My most recent love affair began in September,
Her name is Horchata, and no liquid has been better.

Now all this makes your mouth water,
Your stomach growl but to many it will bring a tear.
As yummy as all this food is, many people,
Especially my favorite people- children,
Will die from hunger and starvation this year.
And because we live in a nation of much wealth,
This crisis will only slightly affect our health,
Our economic health.
You will live today,
Though it may be on PB and J.
I don't say all this shit to bring you down.
I say it cause I want us to respect all we have,
And I like the world to have healthy kids around.
So eat your foods, eat them and live very well.
And when the time comes, you'll be healthy enough to fight back,
And we'll redistribute the wealth...

The Grumpy Couple

I don't want to be the grumpy couple
We don't always have to be talking
Just let's not be grumpy
Let's not be the table that has no words
The table that can't focus on French fries
Cause we're too focused on the…..5 times we've lied to ourselves…In the last 5
minutes … About why we should be together
Why couldn't we be the couple that sat in the car longer…

   Having an 8th grade make out session, holding hands like we meant it…And not
because if we let go, it meant we were letting go
Let's be the couple that looks into each other's eyes
Like we were the only one there
Not seeing the crowds of past trauma
Not seeing the crowds of our past lives
The past times we didn't get it JUST….. Right.
Let's be the couple that even in a busy, fucked up room
We can still find each other's… Eyes, ears, nose … Hands, teeth, face, hair…
LETS BE THE COUPLE THAT GIVES A DAMN!
Let's not be checking our phones for texts from friends or past lovers
Or checking James Franco's Instagram… But why Instagram at all?
Why watch life, when we could live it
Why status update when we could be it
Let's be the couple that wants to be THERE!
Let me be the guy that asks for more water even when I'm not thirsty, but because
I need to sober up, cause I'm drunk on you
Let's be the couple that says 'YES' when they come ask about seeing the dessert
menu
Not because we need that Chocolate Volcano Madness
But because we love madly and it makes us the gladdest to sit at that table longer
Let's SHUT DOWN the restaurant
Let's be the couple the staff cleans up around.
Let's be the couple that says, "let's walk and get Fro-Yo"
Not because we want Fro-Yo
But because we need to know neither of us wants to go home yet

Let's love like it was at first sight
Let's forgive each other every night
Let's not be the grumpy couple
We don't have to say anything all…
But let's just not let it be grumpy.

A Famine of Consciousness

LEAN IN

Across from me on the screens are the screams.
The poor, the hungry, the homeless.
Sex, lies and videotapes.
The streams of the affluent,
Polluted with self-indulgence.

In my chest,
The erratic beats of a welled up blank canvas.
The old man and the sea,
This young man and the community,
A collective, not bargaining,
Instead demanding:
Food, water, shelter
Love…
For my family on the screens, in the streets,
And at the end of the "so it seems…"

New rules are in effect.
They are the laws of Cause and Effect.
No longer will we stand for this universal neglect.
The famine at home is one of Good Sense and Common Decency,
With an abundance of government ignorance and public complacency.
This is a war in Free-ietnam!
Voices raised will create or silence will destroy
Our freedom. Our choices.

Our only choice is…
Freedom.

3/12/12

LEAN IN

The number of times I wrote the date today,
But I am still not sure what it means.
A code to the present day, or just a count?
How dare I count the days?
Do we count our hopes and dreams, because they matter more.
Place value on the past or the muses,
On the anchors or the turbines,
On the kings or the cultures?
All things bare for observation, for new beginnings.
I reread "Words of the Master"
Looking for directions, and
Every page was covered in mirrored glass - Where I could see only truth.
I am ready for my updates to install,
I feel like I have been asleep.
I remember the days,
Lights and shades.
Microphones and pages.
Sitting at the back of The Red Room passing the days.
The number of times I wrote the date today,
But I am still not sure what it means.
The pace of the thoughts around me is quick.
I stop, wait, and see.
Turn to the windows in my mind
Led forward by the words of the master:
        "I believe in the light that shines and will never die"
I turn and bare all to that light.
Slow my pace,
Leave my bags behind.
Because,
All you can carry is not always what you should bring.

She Let You Down

LEAN IN

She let you down,
Sang you to sleep,
Gave you Christmas and joined you for your first light.

Extinguished, left breathless.
Laid a shadow on the present.
Weights of immeasurable magnitudes,
These moist serpents, they travel slowly.
Somewhere I got lost, somewhere
Too suddenly.
This grief is a middle of the road- both lanes facing traffic type feeling,
All too late in the evening…

She let you down,
Sang you to sleep,
Gave you Christmas and joined you for your first light.

They were simple and special,
Unique little words spread on papyrus.
Long gone, but not forgotten as I maneuver through these hills of grief,
The mists of days past remembered.
Scents of shag carpet and a final embrace
At the airport late in the day

She let me down,
Sang me to sleep,
Gave me Christmas…
And joined me for my first light.

Roger

"I can't have my physical freedom"
"It's all by design"
"It's not what they see for me"

Dry eyes, tears in his heart,
I stand 6 feet tall, but feel moused by every
   "Dr. Garry, Please!"
He said, *"I want to talk to my mother, but like this guy over here, she's gone".*
It's his life, 18 in, how many more to go?
It's all in an hour.
Life and death,
Like High and Low Pressure Systems
Combined in a personal, pain, in-group hurricane.
With Sadness Tsunamis,
We wear life preservers of eye contact
Hoping we'll see each other…
Through grief rainstorms, oceans of loss and left behinds.

Sitting, trying to drown out all the lies we were told
About what we were going to grow up to be.
Avoiding mirrors, running from self-fulfilling prophecies.

This is an hour.
60 minutes that CBS
Needs to SEE to BELIEVE there is human-NESS here.

Tears pool up, but it is rare to see a release.
It's a beast.
Cannot believe what I hear or see,
So much greatness,
Beat down,
By the free, those on the street.

Sons, brothers, fathers, uncles
   Locked in,
By beliefs and bars,
By crushed hopes and trauma.

This system is the ninth wonder,
And it's going to take years to get out from under.
In this land of lost and found treasures…

   "It's not what they see for me"
   "It's all by design"
   "I can't have my physical freedom"

He Has a Name

They told you, *"This is what you get."*
You told them, *"I'm not going to let you talk to me like that!"*
They said, *"We don't give a fuck, this is what you get"*,
Your cuffed hands jerked up your back,
This is what you get- Get the Use of Force,
Get used to force- Get this *noose* of course.
This we call justice, is just a farce.
Lame, as a matter of course.
The jailers are the prisoners, and they are just getting worse.
More power is the curse.
They say, *"You're getting smart"*
That is the last thing they want.
Smart, that's how they get hurt.
It's how they get caught – being unjust, being ridiculous,
Seen with disdain and disgust.
This, they call "prison" is a state sponsored suicide.
It's another form of genocide,
The victims are our young men of color,
From this point, it will now be seen as infanticide.
WAIT!
Here is where words collide.
Prison is where worlds collide.
Those with the keys vs. the young men in the community,
Those we gave up on, pissed on and pushed aside.
The dealers and the users, the killers and the abusers,
The ones we ignore when we look in the mirror…
Afraid of the shame and the reoccurring night terrors.
The gift of Unity, that we are all the same,
This responsibility is scary.
So we mimic, shame, and batter away the feeling.
Distance and dehumanize,
Pity, curse, and infantilize.
      And is it any wonder why they *recidivize?*
The training is not for this world of our sons and daughters,
Our sisters and brothers.
It's made of concrete and mortar,
Closed counts and war zones,
Screams and harsh tones,
      "Gladiator training grounds"
Racism, sexism, medical neglect,
Dehumanizing, disrespect for common human rights…
All run rampant.
When we release our brothers and sisters-
They are often worse off than when they arrived.
They came with a heart, a pulse and a soul.
Now our brothers and sisters…
Now they are barely alive.

Rick

March air still stale in my lungs
But things don't really start until you learn to wash your own ass.
And that's why we are all serving life terms with our youth in the blender we call
"prison"
    A place that defies logic.
Where they will let your teeth rot and pull them before they will fix 'em.
    And isn't that how we do the streets-
Low maintenance and then let the justice system pull pieces out…
With guns confused for tasers,
    Batons confused for school supplies,
        Forged scan-trons confused for "No child left behind".
The trail is dirty, littered.
And democracy, like any other social convention,
Is for the weak minded.
No butterfly lies within this cocoon   - Lest we paint her wings with our life's paint
Right now blood, sweat and tears are smeared in the streets
    "The universe may have other plans for you"
But are we prepared for everything we put in our way,
Forgetting that chariots, not iphones will help us travel through this supercollider,
    The battle with the speed of light, with sound in this vacuum
The sterilized version of myself told me I was born again.
A Healthy. Baby. Boy.
This time willing to do it right,
Remember only Love.
    Only the first sip of kombucha,
        The best times with hummingbirds,
            The times I made it through the night,
Meteor showers buy the ocean,
    Spanish over dinner,
        Sitting in the sun and
That these poems be written with tears of joy on evenings with a smile and full
bellies.
    So when the jury, the shadows of what was,
        Returns to measure the changes,
            To bear witness to the last supper and resurrection,
Tea lights will be spread about the ground spelling:
    "Will work for food, a warm bed and love"
This turning of this barge, I call life,
Is page by page,
    Still we are scrawling about in shameless self-promotion.

Begging

We start this eternity with crayons
And a book with beige penguins
Begging for change.
Standing in a field of marigolds
The wind carrying whispers of our mother earth
Begging for change.
Sitting close to the earth
At the low-end of a seesaw
Aching for the taste of the ocean mist
That hangs in the sky above
Begging for change.
Leaning over an oscillating sprinkler
The hose pinched by the weight of a big brother
Begging for change.
We drop all the allusions
All the illusions
And we see the color lines drawn
In our schools and prisons
Begging for change.
In fields plowed over by overdevelopment
Public land eroded by private corporations and selfishness
Begging for change.
Sitting at the bottom of the corporate food chain
401k's eliminated, health care denied, the poor, our youth and elders neglected
Begging for change.
Leaning in, but not too close
Patriotic but Revolutionary
Gripping a pen in a tight fist, begging.
Watching the rotation of
Neglectful leaders, liars and politicians
Begging for Leadership.
Begging for Change.
Begging for Truth.

Those Who Believe

LEAN IN

There are those who believe, To live in peace
Shoot to kill
Shoot to kill
Military minded, small minded
The street is one big land mine
Students act in kind
When taught the repetitive lies
The 'white' kind:
To live in peace
Shoot to kill
Shoot to kill
All in the line of sight
Are those who fight for equal rights
Even waving white flags
You may end up in body bags
It's a shame to live in fear
That last time I checked-
Revolutionaries are killed or jailed every year
Cause to live in peace
Shoot to kill
Shoot to kill
It's far too much for most to bear
So, blinders and ear buds is what they wear
When eyes meet for some connection
It's lost in some distraction
Screens or sex
The "real housewives" or what trend is next.
When the sleepwalkers make a move outside the house
The Federal Pimps turn them out to:
To live in peace
Shoot to kill
Shoot to kill
But all will be awakened by the shouts of the unjustly imprisoned
All shades put away for political reasons
Mumia today, maybe you or me tomorrow
Look at Black August and then choose who to follow
Those who spread democracy, war and devastation
Or the community leaders battling illiteracy and malnutrition
Cause to live in peace
I have the will
You must have the will......

Spoken Word

LEAN IN

To the silence, spoke my soul
Risk, reward
All done, all aboard
Will close my eyes and
Listen for the screams and shouts
Bats in the belfry
Dark sounds
Loud visions
The play on words
Will open the windows
Let the wind in
Stare at the sun
Sing the verses swimming in my mind
Draw blood, Waltz Matilda,
Slip unabated, wishing the days belated
Pound the ground, beat some ass
The world is bow tied, and "I" does matter
Rewarded for my feats
All done
Scored and cut
Hand delivered
To the silence,
Spoke my soul

ABOUT THE AUTHOR

John R. Garry was born and raised in Waterbury, Connecticut.
He is the author of the 2013 release *Regalos de la Isla: Gifts from the Island.*
Living in Oakland, Long Beach and San Luis Obispo California to travels in
Cuba and Spain; his life and travels continue to flavor his performances and
writing. A brother, uncle, godfather, friend, spoken word artist and licensed
psychologist; he makes a practice of connecting with others and finding
only the best within each experience, within each person. When not writing
and performing you will find him gratefully remembering all those who
helped shape the man he is today. He is forever thankful for the journey of
each breath.

www.ingramcontent.com/pod-product-compliance
Lightning Source LLC
Chambersburg PA
CBHW071953100426
42736CB00043B/3206